RIVER
ADVENTURES
NILE RIVER

A+
Smart Apple Media

Published by Smart Apple Media
P.O. Box 3263, Mankato, Minnesota 56002
www.smartapplemedia.com

Published by arrangement with the Watts Publishing
Group LTD, London.

Library of Congress Cataloging-in-Publication Data
Manning, Paul.
  Nile River / Paul Manning.
    p. cm. -- (River adventures)
  Summary: "Traveling from Lake Victoria in Burundi, to
Cairo, Egypt, readers will explore the world's longest river
as they learn about the landscape, ancient civilizations,
and historic landmarks on the Nile, as well as the people
who currently rely on river"--Provided by publisher.
  Includes index.
  ISBN 978-1-59920-917-3 (library binding)
  1. Nile River--Description and travel--Juvenile literature.
2. Nile River Valley--Description and travel--Juvenile
literature. 3. Egypt--Description and travel--Juvenile
literature. 4. Sudan--Description and travel--Juvenile
literature. I. Title. II. Series: River adventures.
  DT115.M37 2015
  916.2--dc23

                                              2012026572

  ISBN: 978-1-59920-917-3   (library binding)
  ISBN: 978-1-62588-587-6   (eBook)

Design, editing and picture research by Paul Manning
Maps by Stefan Chabluk

Printed in the United States by CG Book Printers
North Mankato, Minnesota

PO 1732
3-2015

9 8 7 6 5 4 3 2 1

Note to Teachers and Parents
Every effort has been made to ensure that the websites
listed on page 32 are suitable for children, that they are
of the highest educational value and that they contain no
inappropriate or offensive material. However, because of
the nature of the Internet, it is impossible to guarantee
that the content of these sites will not be altered. We
strongly recommend that Internet access is supervised by
a responsible adult.

Key to images
Top cover image: The Pyramids at Giza near Cairo
Main cover image: Traditional Arab feluccas on the Nile
Previous page: A Nile crocodile swallowing a fish
This page: A panorama of the Nile at Aswan.

Picture Credits
Main cover image, Shutterstock/Mykhaylo Palinchak; small cover image,
Shutterstock/sculpies; 1, Dreamstime/Johan63; 2-3, Shutterstock/Halime
Betin; 4 (map), Stefan Chabluk; 5t, Shutterstock/bestimagesevercom;
5b, Yves Gellie/Corbis; 6, sarahemcc; 7t, Shutterstock/Oleg Znamenskiy;
7b, Shutterstock/Hector Conesa; 8. Dreamstime/Wollwerth; 9b, Steve
Evans; 9t, Dreamstime/Wollwerth; 10, Mohamed Messara/EPA/Corbis;
11t, Kazuyoshi Nomachi/Corbis; 11b, Shutterstock/Joanna Wnuk; 12,
Shutterstock/Imagine Images /Alastair Pidgen; 13t, Petr Adam Dohnálek;
13b, Shutterstock/Urosr; 14, Shutterstock/Nik7ch; 15tl, Giustino; 15tr,
Giustino; 15b, Dreamstime/Edwardje; 16, Brian McMorrow/Pbase/
International Rivers; 17t, Sudani; 17b, Shutterstock/Urosr; 18, Hajor; 19t,
Than217; 19b, Cjbshaw; 20, Shutterstock/Bumihills; 21r, Shutterstock/
Galyna Andrushko; 21l, Shutterstock/Nestor Noci; 25b, Rémih; 22, USAID;
23t, Dreamstime/Stesharp; 24, Marc Ryckaert (MJJR); 25t, Dreamstime/
Zakharchenko; 25b, Karelj; 26, Dreamstime/Baloncici; 27t, Dreamstime/
Baloncici; 27b, Shutterstock/Louise Cukrov; 28, Yves Gellie/Corbis; 29t,
Shutterstock/Baloncici; 29b, Dreamstime/Riaanvdb; 31a, Dreamstime/
Romanvm; 31b, Shutterstock/Christian Lindner; 31c, Dreamstime/
Mareandmare; 31d, Dreamstime/Wisconsinart; 31e, Dreamstime/Matejh;
31f, Dreamstime/Afhunta; 31g, Mahmoudmahdy. .

CONTENTS

A Nile Journey

The Nile is the longest river in the world. From the **source** of the White Nile in Burundi, its water takes six months to reach the sea. You will follow its 4,130-mile (6,650-km) journey from south to north.

A Vital Waterway

For thousands of years, the Nile has been a transportation route, a source of water for farming, and a home for fish, plants, and wildlife. The first people to live on the banks of the Nile were hunters and fishers who settled there 8,000 years ago. By 3000 BC, the ancient Egyptians were living in the Nile Valley, using the river to water their crops. Only 1 inch (2.5 cm) of rain falls in Egypt each year. Without the Nile, all of Egypt would be desert.

Which Nile?

The Nile is really many rivers. Most of its water comes from the Blue Nile. This river starts at Lake Tana in Ethiopia and flows into Sudan from the southeast.

The White Nile is longer than the Blue Nile and is named after the whitish clay that clouds its waters. It rises in Burundi in the Great Lakes region of central Africa, then flows north through Uganda and South Sudan.

The two rivers meet near the Sudanese capital of Khartoum. The river north of Khartoum is sometimes known as the "United Nile."

◄ This traditional Nile sailing boat is called a felucca.

Where is the source?

Since the third century BC, people have tried to find out where the Nile begins. In 1613, the Spanish explorer Pedro Paez discovered Lake Tana in Ethiopia, the source of the Blue Nile. In 1857, the British explorer John Speke traced the White Nile as far south as Lake Victoria. Today, the Nile is measured from the Kagera River and its **tributary**, the Ruvubu, in Burundi.

◄ All along the river, farmers depend on Nile water to grow crops and **irrigate** their fields.

UGANDA

Owen Falls Dam

Lake Victoria

TANZANIA

YOU ARE HERE

Lake Victoria

Your journey begins at Lake Victoria, where the White Nile flows north through Uganda. It's early in the morning, but already the air is hot and steamy as you load up your boat.

Africa's Largest Lake

Along the shore, small fishing boats are getting ready for the day. Lake Victoria is Africa's largest lake, and fishing is a vital industry for the millions who live around it. The Nile perch is Africa's biggest freshwater fish, growing up to 6 feet (1.8 m) long and weighing over 175 pounds (80 kg). Further downstream, the Nile is also home to catfish, eel, lungfish, mudfish, and tiger fish.

▼ Fishermen prepare to leave the shore of Lake Victoria in the early morning to fish for Nile perch.

◀ At Owen Falls Dam, the waters of the Nile are used to produce hydroelectricity for Uganda, Kenya, and Tanzania.

What is hydroelectricity?

Hydroelectric power is energy that is produced by fast-flowing water. A **dam** holds back the flow of the river and forces it through a narrow gap. The quickened flow turns the blades of a giant wheel called a turbine. The turbine drives a generator that produces electricity.

Wildlife Alert!

At Owen Falls Dam, the Nile leaves Lake Victoria and winds north through nearly 310 miles (500 km) of dense forest before reaching the lakes of the Great Rift Valley. There are many dangerous rapids here, so parts of your journey have to be made by road.

As you travel downriver, your guide points out crocodiles and hippos basking on the banks. Crocodiles can be deadly, but more people in Africa are killed by hippos. Male hippos defend their terrritory fiercely, and mothers can be very protective of their young.

▶ During the day, hippos keep cool in the river shallows. At dusk, they leave the river to graze by the water's edge.

The White Nile

As your boat reaches South Sudan, you enter a region of rich grassland and **rain forest**. Far off to the west, isolated hills rise sharply from the flat uplands.

The White Nile

SOUTH SUDAN

Juba

YOU ARE HERE

▼ A Dinka tribesman herds cattle in the grasslands of South Sudan.

A Dinka Village

On the riverbank, you pass a cluster of thatched huts where herdsmen are tending their cattle. These are **nomadic** farmers of the Dinka tribe. Dinka children love their animals and think of them as part of the family. Young Dinka men are even named after the family's favorite oxen, in the hope that they will grow up to be as strong and handsome as them!

A Wandering Life

Mooring your boat in the evening, you meet a group of local farmers who invite you to their village to share a meal. These tribesmen move with their herds to higher ground during the wet season, and return to the river in November when it is dry.

The villagers are hopeful for the future, but after years of war, South Sudan is a desperately poor country. It is several days' journey on foot to the nearest hospital, and many children die before the age of five.

▲ In a village in South Sudan, a woman cooks a meal of **cassava** over a wood fire.

A New Country

For more than 20 years, the people of southern Sudan were at war with the mainly Muslim people from the north. The long conflict led to **famine**, and millions had to leave their homes to avoid starvation. After a **referendum** in 2011, South Sudan broke away from the north to become Africa's newest country.

► These thatched huts by the river are built on stilts to protect them from flooding during the rainy season.

The Great Swamp

Heading north, your boat slows and bumps into an island of papyrus grass. This is the Sudd, one of the largest swamps in the world.

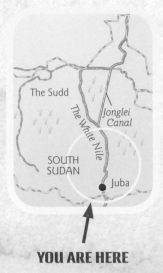

YOU ARE HERE

A Wetland Wilderness

The Sudd has many different habitats, including forest, open water, and grasslands called the **savannah**. Apart from scattered villages, very few people live in this great wilderness.

In the rainy season, vast herds of kob antelope leave the Sudd grasslands and head for drier land. This is one of the most spectacular wildlife **migrations** in Africa.

▼ A boatman ferries passengers across the Nile at Juba in South Sudan.

▶ During the wet season, the Sudd expands to cover nearly 50,200 square miles (130,000 square km). Many animals live here, including elephants, ostriches, leopards, and poisonous snakes.

Floating Islands

In the Sudd, papyrus and other plants soak up the water like a giant sponge. This helps to stop the river from flooding, and takes out some of the mud and tiny stones that the river has picked up along its journey. Eventually, the plants form huge islands that break off and float through the swamp.

Insect Bites

Thick vegetation clogs the water, and this part of your journey is slow. The hot, steamy air is always full of flying insects. At night, you sleep under a mosquito net to avoid being covered in bites.

What is papyrus?

Papyrus is a type of grass that grows by the Nile. It is also the name of a thick papery material made from the stem of the papyrus plant. Papyrus was first used as a writing material by the ancient Egyptians. It is still used today to make boats, mattresses, mats, rope, sandals, and baskets.

◀ Papyrus grows in thick clumps throughout the Sudd region.

YOU ARE HERE

Where Rivers Meet

Nearly 310 miles (500 km) north of the Sudd, you cross the border into Sudan. At the twin cities of Omdurman and Khartoum, the Blue Nile and the White Nile meet.

▼ Khartoum is one of Africa's great crossroads, and a meeting place for people from all over Sudan and beyond.

A Busy Capital

Khartoum is Sudan's capital. It is a busy modern city with offices, banks, and hotels. It is also one of the world's hottest places, with summer temperatures reaching a scorching 118°F (48°C). Where the two rivers join, you can see the different colored waters flowing side by side for a distance before mixing together.

◀ Khartoum's huge street market, the Souq al Arabi, takes up much of the city center. You can buy everything here from pots and pans to bars of gold.

Living by the River

The Nile dominates Khartoum and Omdurman. Crops grown on the **fertile** riverbanks are sold in the cities' markets, and fishing and boat-building are still important to the people there. The river brings many gifts, but it can be a danger too. In 1988, unusually high floods caused the Nile to flood its banks. Many parts of Khartoum were devastated, and thousands were left homeless.

The Nubians

In ancient times, Sudan was part of a region called Nubia. The Nubians once ruled Egypt and built pyramids that can still be seen at Meroë, 125 miles (200 km) north of Khartoum. Today, Nubians live in the area between northern Sudan and southern Egypt.

◀ These Nubian pyramids at Meroë, north of Khartoum, date from the third century BC.

YOU ARE HERE

The Blue Nile

From Khartoum, you travel back upstream to the source of the Blue Nile. It's a long detour—around 995 miles (1,600 km)—but it's worth it to see Lake Tana in Ethiopia and the spectacular Blue Nile Gorge.

▼ Between June and September, heavy rain pours into the Blue Nile Gorge and the river grows into a raging torrent. By the time it reaches Khartoum, it has risen by more than 10 feet (3 m).

Africa's "Grand Canyon"

Your journey takes you deep into the Ethiopian Highlands. At the Blue Nile Gorge, the river carves out a gigantic hollow nearly 3,280 feet (1,000 m) deep in places.

With its steep rocky walls, the **gorge** is home to monkeys, mountain cats, and many rare birds. Some tribes in this remote part of Africa have never seen a European visitor.

▲ Lake Tana is Ethiopia's largest lake. It was formed millions of years ago by a volcanic eruption. About 20 miles (30 km) downstream, the river is stained brown with volcanic **silt** as it plunges over the Tis Issat Falls (right).

The Blue Nile's Source

Lake Tana is a huge **reservoir** for the Blue Nile. From here, torrents of silt-laden water sweep downstream every year in one of the most dramatic river floods in the world.

Today, all is peaceful and calm on the lake. Local fishermen in papyrus canoes called *tankwas* are setting their nets. From the shore, you study the teeming birdlife, which includes fish vultures, hornbills, and flocks of pelicans.

A Dangerous Journey

The Blue Nile is still one of the world's least explored rivers. In 2005, adventurers Les Jickling and Mark Tanner became the first to paddle from the source of the Blue Nile to the Mediterranean Sea in small canoes. Over five months, they survived bandit raids, malaria, and hippo attacks before reaching the Nile delta.

▶ In the Ethiopian Highlands, this young girl fetches water from the Nile every day for washing, cooking, and drinking.

The Cataracts

YOU ARE HERE

Back on the "United Nile," you continue your journey through Sudan. From Khartoum, the Nile veers southwest in a huge arc called the "Great Bend." Along this stretch are the six fast-flowing Nile **cataracts**.

▼ In ancient times, the cataracts prevented people from traveling upstream. The ancient Egyptians never explored beyond this point, and the cataracts marked the limit of their kingdom.

Tectonic Shifts

Both the "Great Bend" and the cataracts were created millions of years ago by giant slabs of rock called tectonic plates shifting beneath the Earth's surface. For most of the year, the Nile cataracts are impassable, but during the flood season, the water level rises and parts of the river can be traveled by boat.

The Merowe Dam

The Merowe Dam in northern Sudan is one of Africa's biggest hydropower plants. The land behind it was once farmed by local people, but was flooded to form the dam reservoir. When this happened, many refused to leave their homes and were forced off their land by the Nile waters.

A Desert Landscape

Around you now is stony desert. During the day, the temperature can rise to 99°F (37°C), but at night it can fall as low as 31°F (−1°C). It hardly ever rains here, and only a narrow strip of land on either side of the river is **habitable**.

Sandstorm!

As your boat continues downriver, your guide points to the sky and warns you to cover your face. There's a sandstorm approaching!

Within minutes, the storm is all around you, blotting out the sun and turning the sky red. After an hour, the wind dies down and the air clears. Sand is everywhere in your clothes and hair, but it's a relief to breathe freely again!

◀ In the desert, people rely on camels for transportation. Camels can travel for up to seven days without water, often carrying heavy loads.

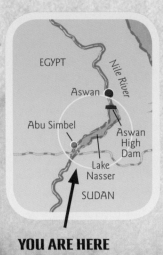

EGYPT

Nile River

Aswan

Abu Simbel

Aswan High Dam

Lake Nasser

SUDAN

YOU ARE HERE

Taming the Flood

North of the Nile's "Great Bend," the river opens out into the vast expanse of Lake Nasser, the biggest man-made lake in the world. At the Aswan High Dam, you enter Egypt.

▼ As well as controlling the Nile flood, the Aswan High Dam generates more than 10 billion kilowatt-hours of electricity every year—enough to power a million televisions for 20 years!

Floods and Famine

Before the dam was built, the annual Nile floods brought vital water to Egypt—but they could bring ruin too. If the flood was too heavy, crops could be wiped out. If the flood was poor, the lack of water caused **drought** and famine.

The Aswan High Dam was completed in 1970 to control the Nile. It allows floodwater to be stored during the rainy season and released in time of drought.

◀ Huge statues guard the entrance to the temple of Rameses II at Abu Simbel.

The Abu Simbel Temples

Overlooking the south side of Lake Nasser are two massive carved temples at Abu Simbel. They are among the great historic sites of Egypt. These twin temples were carved out of the mountainside during the thirteenth century BC as twin monuments to Rameses II and his queen, Nefertari.

When the Aswan High Dam was built, engineers cut the temples into huge chunks and moved them stone by stone to a special hill above the level of the lake to save them from the Nile waters.

The "Key of the Nile"

The ankh, sometimes known as the "key of the Nile," is an ancient Egyptian symbol of eternal life. The oval head is thought to stand for the Nile delta, the vertical section for the course of the river, and the horizontal arms for the west and east of Egypt.

▶ A keeper of the temples at Abu Simbel holds a key in the shape of an ankh.

Aswan to Luxor

YOU ARE HERE

Aswan is Egypt's southernmost city. From now on, the river flows more smoothly, with no more dams or cataracts to slow your journey.

A Market Town

▼ Aswan was once a frontier post between Egypt and Nubia. In ancient times, stone was dug out of the hills here to build the pyramids.

Aswan's streets are lively and crowded, especially on market days. Among the local people, Nubians are easy to spot in their long, flowing clothes. The women's dress is called a *girgar* and is worn with colorful headgear and lots of jewelry. The men wear a full-length white robe called a *galabia* that keeps them cool in the baking sun.

◀ Traders meet to buy and sell camels at Aswan's monthly **livestock** market.

▼ This carved figure of the god Horus can be seen at the temple at Philae, an island on the river near Aswan.

An Island in the Nile

At Aswan, the island of Elephantine was an important trading point on the river. It was also a sacred site for the ancient Egyptians, and the home of Khnum, the god of the cataracts who guarded the waters of the Nile. You stop here to visit the temple and to see the remains of the ancient stone quarries.

▶ In this carved stone tablet, the round-bellied Nile god Hapi is shown offering gifts of food and water.

The Nile Gods

In ancient Egyptian **mythology**, the god Osiris was the bringer of all new life, including the annual flooding of the Nile. In a special festival celebrated during the flood, clay figures of Osiris were planted with barley. The god of the flood was Hapi. He is depicted as a fat figure bringing water and plentiful food.

EGYPT

Upper Nile Valley

Luxor

Aswan

YOU ARE HERE

Farming the Nile

Along the Upper Nile Valley, lush green fields contrast starkly with the barren desert beyond. It's easy to see why Egypt has been called "the gift of the Nile," and why the ancient Egyptians worshiped the river as the source of life itself.

▼ An Egyptian farmer irrigates her crops with water from the Nile.

Irrigation

In the fertile river valley, the fields are irrigated year-round by Nile water. Everywhere you look, farmers are at work growing cereals, fruits, vegetables, and beans. Rice is an important crop for **export**, and Egyptian cotton is sold all over the world. Every available patch of soil is used for growing.

▲ These fields near Luxor in the Upper Nile Valley have been farmed since the time of the ancient Egyptians.

The Shaduf

Many of the farming methods used here go back thousands of years. The water-lifting device known as the shaduf first appeared in the Upper Nile Valley sometime after 1500 BC. Nowadays, it is being replaced by modern diesel or electric pumps, but some farmers (known as fellahin) still use shadufs to irrigate their fields.

The Egyptian Calendar

In ancient Egypt, there were three seasons. Akhet, the flooding season, lasted from June to September. Peret (October to February) was the growing season, when the floods drained away, leaving a layer of rich, black soil. In Shemu (March to May), the fully grown crops were harvested.

▶ This ancient Egyptian wall painting shows a farmer using a shaduf to lift water.

From Luxor to Cairo

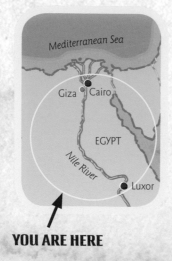

YOU ARE HERE

At Luxor, the river becomes a busy tourist route. From now on, your journey will take you past many of the most famous sights of Egypt.

The Valley of the Kings

Where Luxor stands today, the ancient Egyptian city of Thebes once stood on both sides of the river. On the east bank was the "city of the living," with great temples and palaces. On the west bank was the Valley of the Kings, containing the tombs of the Pharaohs, including Tutankhamun.

Modern Luxor has been called the greatest open-air museum in the world. Often there are more tourists in the town than locals.

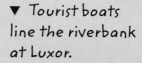

▼ Tourist boats line the riverbank at Luxor.

◄ The pyramids were giant tombs for the Pharaohs. Sites were chosen on the west of the Nile because it was believed that the home of the dead was toward the setting sun.

The Pyramids of Giza

North of Luxor are the towns and cities where most Egyptians now live. This stretch of the river is also where most of the great historical sites of ancient Egypt are to be found.

At 479 feet (146 m) high, the Pyramid of Khufu at Giza, south of Cairo, is the largest of all Egypt's 80 pyramids. For nearly 4,000 years it was the tallest building in the world, until the 525-foot (160 m) spire of Lincoln cathedral was built in England in the thirteenth century.

Tourism on the Nile

Historic sites such as the pyramids and the Valley of the Kings attract visitors from all over the world. The money they spend in shops and hotels is very important to Egypt. Many tourists travel the Nile in luxury cruise ships. Others prefer the gentler pace of a traditional felucca sailing boat.

► A cruiser carries tourists on a sightseeing trip down the Nile.

Cairo

YOU ARE HERE

You have now reached Cairo, the capital of Egypt and a vital trading and business center. Many key industries are based here, from textiles and chemicals to trucks and cars.

Old and New

With a population of more than 17 million, Cairo is Africa's second largest city. Most people who live here are Muslim, and hundreds of **mosques** with tall towers called **minarets** can be seen among the high-rise offices and shopping malls. From the minarets, Muslim religious leaders called *muezzin* can be heard five times a day, calling the faithful to prayer.

▼ *The Nile runs through the center of Cairo, Egypt's capital.*

Old Cairo

On the Nile's east bank are the neighborhoods of Cairo's Islamic quarter. This area is known for its narrow streets and crowded markets. To the south is Old Cairo, home of some of the city's most famous historic buildings.

A Life on the River

Most of Cairo's inhabitants live in apartment blocks on the outskirts of the city, but at el-Tahrir bridge, groups of Nile fishermen and their families still live in boats moored on the river. All year long, it is warm enough to sit outside at night, and many boat-dwellers sleep under the stars.

▶ In Old Cairo, an Egyptian woman bakes pita bread in a traditional brick oven.

▼ On the edges of the city, new suburbs are being built all the time to house Cairo's growing population.

Air Pollution

Like many big cities, Cairo suffers from high levels of air pollution. There are an estimated 4.5 million vehicles on the streets, and the fumes create a blanket of **smog** over the city. Somewhere between 10,000 and 25,000 people a year die of illnesses linked to air pollution.

Mediterranean Sea
Nile Delta
Damietta River
Alexandria
Port Said
Rosetta River
Cairo
Suez Canal
Nile River

YOU ARE HERE

The Nile Delta

Your journey ends at the Nile Delta. Here, the river divides into two main branches, the Damietta and Rosetta. They flow through a giant basin of low-lying marshland before draining into the sea.

▼ The delta's low-lying fields are ideal for rice-growing, but are slowly being poisoned by salt water from the Mediterranean Sea and overuse of chemical **fertilizers**.

Under Threat

Before the Aswan Dam was built, the Nile delta was one of Africa's most fertile regions. Today, rising sea levels are turning it into a salty wasteland. The soil here was once rich and brown, fed by the silt carried downriver by the Nile. Now saltwater is pushing up through the surface, killing plants and threatening the livelihood of local farmers.

▶ Alexandria on the Mediterranean coast may soon be completely cut off from the mainland by rising seawater.

Too Many People

The human pressures on the delta are mounting. About half of Egypt's 88 million people already live in the region, and the numbers are growing all the time. There are not enough houses or jobs for all the people who want to live here.

Flora and Fauna

Although the land is crowded, the delta is still a haven for plants and wildlife. During autumn, parts of the river are red with lotus flowers. Large numbers of water birds spend the winter in the delta, including the world's largest population of little gulls and whiskered terns. Other birds that migrate here are gray herons, Kentish plovers, and cormorants.

A Crowded Region

In Egypt, most people live in a narrow strip of land beside the Nile River. As the population grows, more and more people are forced to settle in the delta. Having so many people in such a small area causes overcrowding everywhere. Schools, hospitals, and other services in the delta region are struggling to cope.

▶ Whiskered tern from Europe are regular winter visitors to the Nile Delta.

Glossary

cassava a protein-rich root crop

cataract a waterfall or stretch of fast-flowing water

dam a barrier that holds back the flow of a river

delta the mouth of a river where it drains into the sea

drought a time when there is very little water

export a product or service that is sold to other countries

famine a time when food is scarce and many people may starve

fertile good for growing

fertilizer chemical used to make soil better for growing

gorge a deep river valley with steep rocky sides

habitable suitable as a home for people

irrigate to water fields or crops to make up for lack of rain

livestock farm animals such as cattle or goats

malaria a disease carried by mosquitoes

migration the movement of large numbers of people or animals from place to place

minaret the tall tower of a mosque from which a priest calls people to prayer

mosque a Muslim place of worship

mythology beliefs or stories about gods or heroes

nomadic people who travel from place to place with herds of grazing animals

rain forest dense, humid forest found in tropical regions

referendum a vote that is held to decide an important issue

reservoir a lake that is used to store water

savannah grassy plain found in tropical and subtropical regions

silt fine sand or clay carried downstream by a river

smog thick haze caused by air pollution

source the beginning of a river, usually a lake or spring

tributary a stream or river that flows into another bigger one

Nile Quiz

Look up the information in this book or online. Find the answers on page 32.

1 Match the captions to the pictures.

1

2

3

4

5

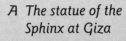
6

A *The statue of the Sphinx at Giza*

B *The Tis Issat Falls on the Blue Nile*

C *A felucca sailboat on the Nile at Aswan*

D *A date palm*

E *An African fish eagle*

F *A man wearing traditional Arab headdress*

2 These places can all be found along the Nile. Place them in the right order, starting with the ones nearest to the Mediterranean Sea:

Khartoum
Lake Nasser
Port Said
Cairo
Aswan
Lake Tana

3 True or false?

The Blue Nile is named that because silt turns its waters almost black. In Sudanese, the words for blue and black are the same.

4 This ancient Nile barge known as the Khufu Ship is now preserved in a Cairo museum. Do you know where it was found and how old it might be?

Websites and Further Reading

Websites

- *www.socialstudiesforkids.com/articles/geography/nileriver.htm*
  Useful facts and figures about the Nile River.

- *www.mummies2pyramids.info/geography-cities/facts-about-nile.htm*
  Fascinating facts about the ancient Egyptians and the Nile River.

Further Reading

Banting, Erinn. *Nile River* (Wonders of the World). Weigl, 2014.

Bojang, Ali Brownlie. *Egypt in our World* (Countries in our World). Smart Apple Media, 2012.

Simon, Charnan. *The Secrets of the Nile* (Geography of the World). The Child's World, 2014.

Index

Answers to Nile Quiz

1 1E, 2C, 3A, 4F, 5B, 6D. **2** Port Said, Cairo, Aswan, Lake Nasser, Khartoum, Lake Tana. **3** True. **4** The Khufu Ship was found buried at the foot of the Great Pyramid of Giza. It is believed to be more than 4,500 years old.